Sustainable refurbishment of Victorian housing

Guidance, assessment method and case studies

Tim Yates
Technical Director
Heritage and Stone, BRE Construction Division

This work has been partly funded by BRE Trust. Any views expressed are not necessarily those of BRE Trust. While every effort is made to ensure the accuracy and quality of information and guidance when it is first published, BRE Trust can take no responsibility for the subsequent use of this information, nor for any errors or omissions it may contain.

The mission of BRE Trust is 'Through education and research to promote and support excellence and innovation in the built environment for the benefit of all'. Through its research programmes the Trust aims to achieve:

- a higher quality built environment
- built facilities that offer improved functionality and value for money
- a more efficient and sustainable construction sector, with
- a higher level of innovative practice.

A further aim of the Trust is to stimulate debate on challenges and opportunities in the built environment.

BRE Trust
Garston, Watford, Herts WD25 9XX, UK
Tel: 01923 664598,
secretary@bretrust.co.uk
www.bretrust.org.uk
www.bre.co.uk

BRE Trust publications are available from
www.ihsbrepress.com
or
IHS BRE Press
Willoughby Road
Bracknell RG12 8FB
Tel: 01344 328038
Fax: 01344 328005
Email: brepress@ihsatp.com

Requests to copy any part of this publication should be made to the publisher:
IHS BRE Press
Garston, Watford WD25 9XX
Tel: 01923 664761
Email: brepress@ihsatp.com

FB14

Acknowledgements

The project was funded by the BRE Trust. Many BRE staff contributed to the report, amongst these were Martin Cook, Stephen Garvin, Robin Hall, John Houston, Simon Nicol, David Richardson, Keith Thomson and Alan Yates.

I am also very grateful for the support from those involved in the three case study projects – Istekar Bokhari (Pendle Borough Council), Sylvia Wilson (Whitefield Conservation Action Group), James Hulme (The Prince's Foundation for the Built Environment), Penney Poyzer (Nottingham Ecohome) and Liz Warren (Flagship Project).

Photographs which do not bear an attribution were taken specifically for the project.

EcoHomes is a Registered Trade Mark of BRE.

Contents

Preface

This project has its origin in the discussions that ensued after the publication of the *40% House* report by Oxford Environmental Change Institute in 2005. The report again put into public debate the potential conflict between the need to meet environmental targets, particularly carbon dioxide emissions, whilst retaining our traditional urban landscape and so re-using the resources – materials and energy – that had gone into their construction. The situation is made more complex by the need to take into account the wishes of the communities that live in the traditional housing found in many urban and rural areas and to achieve this within a market driven economic system.

From these background considerations the idea of the development of a methodology for the assessment of the different interventions was put to the BRE Trust who agreed to fund the 12 month project from which this report is the output. The method used for the comparison of different options is based on EcoHomes, a rating method for new, converted or renovated homes, which covers both houses and apartments, which has been developed by BRE and proved over many years.

This report is aimed towards those involved in deciding on the viability of regeneration and refurbishment projects in pre-1919 housing. It provides guidance on assessing different options for interventions and defines limits which need to be considered in examining the viability of these options – in terms of conservation, environment, economics and social needs. It illustrates some of the different approaches that have been tried through case studies in Nelson, London and Nottingham.

The report does not contain all of the details of the assessment scoring but it is expected that these will be available via the BRE website during Autumn 2006.

Tim Yates
BRE

September 2006

Introduction

Continued use, re-use and restoration of housing dating from the period between 1840 and 1919 (referred to in this report as Victorian) represents a unique set of opportunities but also a number of associated risks. It is believed that over 50% of expenditure in the UK construction industry relates to the repair, refurbishment and maintenance of the existing building stock and, with the greater emphasis on the sustainability of urban areas, this is likely to increase. The risks to be managed include working practices, and the durability, reliability and maintainability of materials which are at some undetermined point in their expected lifetime during refurbishment and subsequent occupation. Current practice and advice are primarily aimed at new build and modern building fabrics. With the growing emphasis on re-use and regeneration of the built heritage there is a need to evaluate the costs and benefits related to modern building practice against the occupancy and use of Victorian and Edwardian housing, and to do this in the light of requirements for materials, durability and whole building performance.

The number of houses dating from this period represents a significant proportion of the current housing stock. In 2004 the total number of households in the UK was estimated to be 25.3 million and some 17% of the dwellings were constructed before 1919 – some 4.3 million houses many of which will date from between 1840 and 1919.

More detailed information on the pre-1919 housing stock in England can be obtained from the English House Condition Survey (EHCS): www.communities. gov.uk/index.asp?id=1155269. This includes costs for general repair which show that older houses are, as expected, more expensive to repair – reflecting the greater amount of work required.

The potential conflicts between requirements for modern houses and the performance of older houses have been highlighted in a number of high profile projects. An example is the redevelopment in Nelson, Lancashire where the local authority's decision to demolish more than 400 of the existing 19th century houses in the Whitefield area was successfully challenged by the occupants with the support of English Heritage and the Prince's Foundation. A second example occurred in 2005 when many conservation groups raised concerns at the large-scale demolition plans of the then Office of the Deputy Prime Minister, which seemed to indicate a lack of joined-up thinking on sustainability and sustainable communities. These concerns were further highlighted by the publication in 2005 of the *40% House* report (www.eci.ox. ac. uk/ lowercf/40house.html) which advocated the demolition of up to 8 million houses, including a very large proportion of those constructed before 1919.

Table 1 Types of accommodation by construction date in the United Kingdom in 2004–2005 (percentages)						
	Before 1919	1919–1944	1945–1964	1965–1984	1985 or later	All
House or bungalow						
Detached	14	11	15	27	33	100
Semi-detached	10	25	29	23	14	100
Terraced	29	16	20	24	12	100
Flat or maisonette						
Purpose-built	6	9	24	35	25	100
Conversion	66	20	7	4	3	100
All dwellings*	17	17	21	25	20	100

* Includes other types of accommodation, such as mobile homes.
Source: *General household survey*, Office for National Statistics, *Continuous household survey*, Northern Ireland Statistics and Research Agency.

These figures need to be seen in the context that more than 80,000 dwellings per annum were demolished under slum clearance powers in the early 1970s, but this fell to some 4200 in 1992, an annual replacement rate of less than one in every 4750 dwellings.

The situation is clearly complex, with competing demands, and so it is essential to evaluate the various options and determine a way forward that produces the overall lowest environmental impact in that particular time and place. To be sustainable these need to be evaluated and considered alongside the whole life cost for each option, and the societal impacts and benefits of any proposed redevelopment, whether as new build or refurbishment.

This report has been prepared as part of a project undertaken by the construction consultancy team at BRE with support from the Centre for Sustainable Construction at BRE. It builds on the work already undertaken for English Heritage in relation to the discussions on the *40% House* report and for the European Union as part of the CultStrat project (www.corr-institute.se/cultstrat). It also builds on the work reported in BRE Information Paper IP9/02 on sustainable refurbishment (Anderson and Mills, 2002) which was developed as a methodology and tool (Office Scorer) for assessing the choice between refurbishing and redeveloping office buildings. IP9/02 concluded that, typically, refurbishment is lower in both environmental and whole life cost impacts than redevelopment. EcoHomes XB is an environmental assessment tool launched in June 2006 which can be applied to the refurbishment of domestic housing, and which enables decision making to take account of a wide range of key issues relating to the built environment.

The present BRE project has been running in parallel with the University of Reading's College of Estate Management's (CEM) project on sustainable house building. The two projects will complement each other, with the BRE project concentrating on the development of a robust methodology for assessing pre-1919 properties and supporting this with guidance, and the CEM project producing data on the development of long term costing of refurbishment and sustainability.

The key objective of the BRE project was to formulate a method of assessing Victorian house refurbishment similar to that used in EcoHomes. This was seen as realistic because of the comparatively small number of typologies that housing of this era fits into – brick or stone-built terraced housing on two, three or four levels.

The objectives of the project were to:
● evaluate the refurbishment/conversion of traditionally built housing dating from 1840–1919, looking specifically at competing requirements for modern energy and acoustic standards, whole building performance and the effects of durability, reliability and maintainability of the building fabric
● examine the economic, environmental and social costs and benefits of retaining this part of the building stock
● develop a methodology that can be used in the assessment process.

Background to refurbishing sustainable Victorian housing

Considerable redevelopment of urban housing in the UK has been carried out since the 1980s. In many cases the regeneration programmes have seen existing buildings demolished and replaced by new build housing. However, the refurbishment of existing buildings may be a cost effective choice, and in many ways is a more desirable option. Such refurbishment can result in better quality housing for the occupiers, and reduced heat losses and it also retains the fabric of the structure along with the traditional urban landscape that forms such an important part of our built heritage.

In some locations, particularly in historic city centres, the refurbishment of properties is a well established feature of housing regeneration, and successful refurbishment of many traditional and more modern buildings has been achieved, although undoubtedly there have been problems with some projects. This may be simply because refurbishment work of a building brings with it particular problems which are not encountered with new build, or it may involve problems unique to regeneration in urban areas.

A recent feature of housing refurbishment is the regeneration of waterfront locations. This is taking place throughout the UK in cities such as Liverpool, Cardiff and Belfast. Much of the regeneration work has involved the refurbishment of older buildings, particularly for use as luxury flats or in the leisure sector. A driver for much of this work has been to help provide housing close to the city centre but it does, to some extent, ignore the spatial and social patterns typical of inner city areas.

There are countless examples of Victorian housing converted from single-family occupancies into multi-residential units that demonstrates the flexibility of this type of property to meet the demands of changing demographic patterns and the trend towards smaller households. There are also exemplary case studies of Victorian terraced housing that have been refurbished to high standards of energy efficiency. Achievable standards of sustainable refurbishment of the existing housing stock can be benchmarked against current Building Regulations and EcoHomes ratings for new build.

A great deal of the guidance and case studies produced under the government's Energy Efficiency Best Practice Programme (now continued by the Energy Saving Trust [EST]) concerned Victorian housing refurbishment. Notable summaries were published in the 1990s, for example, Good practice case studies (GPCS) 315 *Energy efficient refurbishment of solid walled houses* and GPCS 316 *Energy efficient refurbishment of solid walled flats*. More recent publications include Good practice guide (GPG) 155 *Energy efficient refurbishment of existing housing* and GPCS 418 *Energy efficient refurbishment of existing housing – case studies*.

In addition, a number of studies of terraced and semi-detached Victorian and Edwardian properties refurbished using integrated packages of measures incorporating insulation, ventilation and efficient heating were documented by BRE in the late 1990s.

Refurbishment of solid walled houses can achieve SAP ratings (Standard Assessment Procedure – the government's standard method of home energy rating) equal to, or better than, those of new build properties complying with Building Regulations.

The energy efficient measures most often adopted in solid walled houses are:
- loft insulation
- insulated dry lining to external walls, or external insulating render
- ground floor insulation
- secondary glazing
- gas central heating with condensing boiler
- factory insulated hot water cylinder
- controlled ventilation system.

Other benefits not related to energy efficiency include:
- reduced maintenance costs due to fewer condensation problems
- higher rental income
- management costs savings
- increased property values.

The potential for energy saving in an older property can be seen in the following example carried out in the mid-1990s in Scotland and the more recent Flagship Project in London (see case study 2 later on page 27).

Refurbishment of a four-storey tenement in Greenock, Scotland

This project was carried out by a housing association in 1996 and involved the full refurbishment and upgrading of a four-storey tenement building. The block was a mixture of one, two and three bedroom flats and during the refurbishment some remodelling was undertaken which reduced the number of flats from 51 to 48. Twenty-two of the flats were privately owned. External walls were solid sandstone and the ground floor is of solid construction. Heating was by gas and electric fires.

The housing association had experience of refurbishing 13 other tenement blocks. As a result they had their own general specification for tenement refurbishment, which the project architects used as a basis for their design (Table 2).

Table 2 Specification for the refurbishment of a tenement in Greenock, Scotland		
Item	Before refurbishment	After refurbishment
Roof	Uninsulated	150 mm mineral wool loft insulation between joists, 50 mm laid over joists
External walls	600 mm sandstone	Plaster removed. External wall – 50 mm expanded polystyrene insulation – plasterboard
Partion walls	Uninsulated	Composite board comprising 12.5 mm wallboard and 19 mm extruded polystyrene fitted internally
Windows	Single glazing	Replacement timber windows with double glazing (22 mm air gap) and draught sealing
Heating	Gas and electric fires	Gas fires, gas fired central heating from back boiler, programmer, room thermostat and thermostatic radiator valves
Hot water	Immersion heaters	Back boiler, 135 litre hot water tank with 80 mm factory applied insulation

Refurbishment specification
The measures included in the final specification were:
- mineral wool loft insulation
- internal insulation and plasterboard to external walls
- insulation to close walls and ceiling
- replacement timber frame double glazing

- kitchen and bathroom extract fans
- draught sealing of front doors of flats
- full gas fired central heating with back boiler (housing association owned flats)
- full gas fired central heating with combination boiler (privately owned flats).

SAP ratings, energy costs and CO_2 emissions

A SAP analysis was carried out for the flats before and after refurbishment. The results from the two flat types estimated to have the highest and the lowest SAP rating after refurbishment are given in Table 3. The analysis showed that good SAP ratings were achieved. Annual space and water heating costs were estimated to have reduced by 64% and 62% for the second floor three-bed flat and the ground floor two-bed flat respectively. CO_2 emissions were estimated to have reduced by 20% and 27%.

Table 3 Estimated SAP ratings, energy costs and CO_2 emissions before and after refurbishment

Item	Second floor three-bed mid flat		Ground floor two-bed gable flat	
	Before	After	Before	After
SAP rating	50	86	23	57
Annual space and water heating costs	£477	£173	£631	£241
CO_2 emissions (tonnes/year)	5.5	4.4	6.7	4.9

Note: The figures are for flats with a back boiler. The substitution of combination boilers in place of back boilers had a minimal effect on these figures, including SAP ratings which increased by only two points. All costs are at 2000 prices.

Problems encountered during the refurbishment works

The clerk of works, interviewed shortly after work was completed, reported that there had been no real buildability problems with the project. The main problem related to the position of the new boilers. The housing association preferred to fit back boilers in tenement flats because this does not require internal space and ventilation is simpler (ie via chimney flues). Other boiler types have to be vented via an external wall and in some flats there can be difficulties in finding such a position. Finding a suitable internal space for the boiler can also be problematic.

The architect was also interviewed. The main problem he reported was that during construction, dampness was found in the cellars and tanking had been required. Repairs to the external stonework had also been undertaken, but this was regarded as quite expected for such a job.

The housing association's views

The housing association's development officer was asked for his views on the project, both just after its completion and four years later in July 2000. After the project had just been completed the housing association was pleased with the refurbishment work. The mixed ownership of the block had caused delays, principally in terms of different specifications and administration work for such matters as access to flats and cost distribution. However, the delays were not significant.

The comments made in July 2000 were also positive. The tenement had been relatively maintenance free and both tenants and owners appeared to be happy with the refurbished property. The major difference to the specification, which in hindsight might have been made, was to install more energy efficient boilers. While this would have reduced household energy costs, there would have been the drawback of loss of space internally because the option of using back boiler would not have been available.

Developing an assessment methodology

The ten years since the mid-1990s have seen considerable development in the ideas associated with regeneration and the requirements have moved far beyond the simple desire to reduce energy consumption. There are now many other aspects of sustainability that need to be taken into account and all of this must be seen against the needs of the people who occupy, or who will occupy, the refurbished houses and the wider economic and social revival of any particular location.

From the outset of the project it seemed logical to adapt the existing EcoHomes system to cover the refurbishment and conservation of buildings which are considered an important part of the landscape but where demolition is often seen as the most practical short term commercial option. The assessment methodology described in this report draws on the most relevant elements of both EcoHomes 2005 and in the EcoHomes XB guidance– *The environmental rating for existing housing* (2006), and it is then supplemented by some units specific to this type of property.

The assessment method uses a scoring system similar to that in the EcoHomes schemes to provide some guidance on the most beneficial actions in terms of impact and, in very general terms, the economic cost.

Development of EcoHomes XB

The Housing Corporation commissioned BRE to develop EcoHomes XB, as an environmental assessment tool for the maintenance and small-scale refurbishment of existing buildings. The scheme was launched in June 2006. EcoHomes XB is based on EcoHomes, which expresses environmental performance on a four-point scale from pass to excellent. (See BRE factsheet www.bre.co.uk/pdf/013.pdf: see also www.breeam.org/ecohomes).

EcoHomes XB is designed to operate on two levels:
- The basic level is for use as an in-house, desktop operation drawing on data already held by the stockholder either in stock registers or other surveys. It is designed to assess large areas of housing such as districts, postal areas etc. At this level the information drawn from Ecohomes XB can be used to highlight problem areas of poor performance, indicating that attention is needed and that an advanced level appraisal is required.
- The advanced level requires more information, some of which may necessitate site visits and SAP data if not already available. This level is designed for discrete groups of houses such as streets or small groups of a single house type. The advanced level will help identify small clusters of dwellings that are in need of priority attention. This level could also be applied to individual buildings if there is sufficient interest in assessing their potential for improvement.

EcoHomes XB has been developed to be easy to use, drawing on data that is either already to hand or readily accessible from other surveys, requiring the minimum amount of additional work and data gathering.

The scoring system for EcoHomes XB is structured in a way that will allow improvements to be measured incrementally, so that even relatively minor improvements will be reflected in the score.

EcoHomes XB allows those responsible for buildings to:

- develop stock profiles in terms of the current environmental performance of their housing
- identify areas of housing that have a poor environmental performance
- target improvements to gain the most environmental benefit
- measure and monitor the progress of their stock.

The two levels of the scheme allows building owners to quickly identify stock which under-performs in environmental terms (basic level). It then allows them to consider measures to improve performance (advanced level).

These ideas can be directly extended to the built heritage and can be made more appropriate by the addition of a category to reflect the use of good practice conservation policy, EcoHomes XBC – the 'C' denoting conservation. EcoHomes XBC should be capable of identifying the limits of improvement which allow the important aspects of the build heritage to be retained whilst maximising the improvements in environmental performance.

Developing EcoHomes XBC for the built heritage

Comparison of baseline scenarios

EcoHomes XBC contains 28 categories which provide a total of 100 credits – the categories cover management, energy, transport, pollution, water, ecology, heating, waste and materials. The selected areas and criteria for the awarding of credits emphasise the need to consider the regeneration of the locality and the management/governance of the areas and not just the changes to a single property – though it is possible to apply the scheme to a single building if required. An additional category has been added to the management area giving an additional ten credits to emphasise the importance of applying good conservation principles to a project, using appropriately qualified companies, and appropriate sustainable materials. It takes into account both the refurbishment stage and the performance of the properties in use. This report also looks at the need to consider environmental benefits against the costs and benefits to society, and the economic implications of a regeneration scheme since these are all integral to truly sustainable regeneration in urban or rural areas.

The Neighbourhood Renewal Unit (NRU) (part of the Department for Communities and Local Government) provides guidance and support on the renewal of communities. It states that "Neighbourhood renewal is about reversing the spiral of decline in our most disadvantaged communities. It involves working from the grassroots to deliver economic prosperity and jobs, safer communities, good education, decent housing and better health, as well as fostering a new sense of community among residents." Further information on the NRU can be found at www.neighbourhood.co.uk.

In addition, it has the potential to allow a number of options to be considered and the best combination of cost, sustainability and conservation of the built environment to be determined. This compensates for the reduced ability to moderate factors affecting environmental performance in existing stock compared with new developments.

The categories covered by the current scheme and the credits available under each heading are outlined in Table 4. Table 4 includes four scenarios, which give an indication of the credits that can be gained through realistic improvements in the locality and the house(s). The scenarios are based on several adjacent streets of late Victorian terraced houses within an urban area.

Scenario 1: The house(s) and area as currently found.
Scenario 2: The same house(s) with the area improved as part of a regeneration plan.
Scenario 3: The house(s) refurbished but with no regeneration of the area
Scenario 4: The house(s) refurbished and the area improved as part of a regeneration plan.

Area	Description	Total number of credits available	Scenario 1 No refurbishment	Scenario 2 Regeneration of locality	Scenario 3 Refurbishment of the houses	Scenario 4 Refurbishment and regeneration
	Table 4 Applying the EcoHomes XBC scoring to four different regeneration scenarios					
Management 1	Energy policy	3	0	3	0	3
Management 2	Energy efficiency	2	0	2	0	2
Management 3	Environmental policy	2	0	2	0	2
Management 4	Tenant consultation	2	0	1	0	2
Management 5	Energy labelled appliances	2	0	1	2	2
Management 6	Conservation policy	5	0	0	5	5
Management 7	Policy on the use of appropriate sustainable materials	5	0	3	5	5
	Management total	**16**	**0**	**12**	**12**	**21**
Energy 1	Carbon dioxide emissions	10	0	0	[6]	[6]
Energy 2	Heating system controls	2	0	1	2	2
Energy 3	Energy and fabric performance	10	0	0	[6]	[6]
Energy 4	Drying space	1	1	1	1	1
Energy 5	External lighting	2	0	2	1	2
	Energy total	**25**	**1**	**4**	**16**	**17**
Transport 1	Public transport	2	2	2	2	2
Transport 2	Cycle storage	2	1	1	2	2
Transport 3	Local amenities	3	2	3	2	3
	Transport total	**7**	**5**	**6**	**6**	**7**
Pollution 1	NOx emissions	3	0	0	3	3
	Pollution total	**3**	**0**	**0**	**3**	**3**
Water 1	Internal water use	5	0	0	5	5
Water 2	External water use	1	1	1	1	1
	Water use total	**6**	**1**	**1**	**6**	**6**
Ecology 1	Ecological enhancement	1	0	1	1	1
Ecology 2	Protection of ecological features	1	0	1	1	1
	Ecology total	**2**	**0**	**2**	**2**	**2**
Health 1	External private space	1	1	1	1	1
Health 2	Internal private space	1	0	0	1	1
Health 3	Controlled ventilation	1	0	0	1	1
	Health total	**3**	**1**	**1**	**3**	**3**
Waste 1	Reduction of refurbishment waste	3	0	3	0	3
Waste 2	Domestic recycling facilities	6	2	2	6	6
Waste 3	Safe disposal of appliances which contain ozone depleting substances	1	1	1	1	1
	Waste total	**10**	**3**	**6**	**7**	**10**
Materials 1	Refurbishment timber – basic building elements	6	0	0	6	6
Materials 2	Refurbishment timber – finishing elements	3	0	0	3	3
Materials 3	Refurbishment – environmental impact of materials	14	0	0	[10]	[10]]
	Materials total	**23**	**0**	**0**	**19**	**19**
	Overall total	**100**	**11**	**32**	**74**	**88**
	EcoHomes rating		**Unrated**	**Poor**	**Very good**	**Excellent**

Figures in squared brackets in Table 4 are ones which it is difficult to estimate and which could vary considerably between different projects.

It should be noted that the regeneration of the area is envisaged as an initiative led by a local authority/registered social landlord including improvements in local administration/management and local transport. The refurbishment of the house(s) is envisaged as a basic upgrading but without any substantial structural work and within conservation guidelines for the retention of the appearance of a locality/area.

From Table 4 it appears that most houses dating from before 1919 will probably be unrated – that it is below Poor. A regeneration scheme that does not address the refurbishment of the houses cannot hope to increase the rating to Better than Poor. The refurbishment of the house alone can potentially increase the rating to Good although this will depend very much on the improvement in energy efficiency of the heating system and the improvement of the fabric, since these will control the energy used and the carbon dioxide emitted. This type of improvement may well require the replacement of windows and the provision of internal or external insulation systems. If the building is in a conservation area or is a listed building then this could prove difficult.

Defining benchmarks for pre-1919 housing using EcoHomes XBC

It is important that the assessment system is capable of defining certain benchmarks – both in terms of the actions taken, the interventions made and the maximum EcoHomes XBC credits for each of these actions. It is also possible to identify a number of limits – that is the extent of changes that can be made or are required without compromising required regulations, principles or best practice. This concept is illustrated in Figure 1 with a number of actions (interventions) and defined limits.

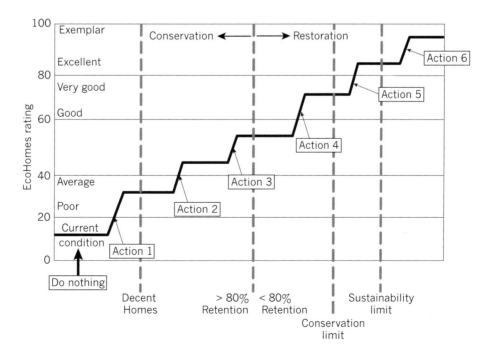

Figure 1 Consequences of actions in the refurbishment of buildings and the determination of limits of intervention showing the EcoHomes rating on the left

Conservation limit

This is defined as the extent to which the building and locality can be changed or altered without compromising conservation principles and best practice. Conservation principles are summarised in a number of charters (for example the Burra Charter [www.icomos.org/australia/burra.html] and the Stirling Charter (www.historic-scotland.gov.uk/stirlingcharter) but they can be summarised as follows:

- the historic environment is a shared resource
- it is essential to understand and sustain what is valuable in the historic environment
- everyone can make a contribution
- understanding the values of places is vital
- places should be managed to sustain their significance
- decisions about change must be reasonable and transparent
- it is essential to document and learn from decisions.

(Taken from *Conservation principles for the sustainable management of the historic environment*, English Heritage, 2005.)

In this case the following definitions have been used:

Conservation: The process of managing change in ways that will best sustain the values of a place in its contexts, and which recognises opportunities to reveal and reinforce those values.

Historic environment: All aspects of the environment resulting from the interaction between people and places through time.

Significance: The sum of the cultural and natural heritage values of a place.

Value: An aspect of worth or importance, in this context ascribed by people to places. Where value can be further broken down into:

> *Aesthetic value*: Relating to the ways in which people respond to a place through sensory and intellectual experience of it.
> *Community value*: Relating to the meanings of a place for the people who identify with it, and whose collective memory it holds.
> *Evidential value*: Relating to the potential of a place to yield primary information about past human activity.
> *Historical value*: Relating to the ways in which a place can provide direct links to past people, events and aspects of life.
> *Instrumental value*: Economic, educational, recreational and other benefits which exist as a consequence of the cultural or natural heritage values of a place.

(Adapted from *Conservation principles for the sustainable management of the historic environment*, English Heritage, 2005.)

One of the most relevant documents to refer to when considering the refurbishment of Victorian and Edwardian terraced housing is the International Committee on Monuments and Sites (ICOMOS) Charter on the Built Vernacular Heritage (1999). The introduction states:

> "The built vernacular heritage occupies a central place in the affection and pride of all peoples. It has been accepted as a characteristic and attractive product of society. It appears informal, but nevertheless orderly. It is utilitarian and at the same time possesses interest and beauty. It is a focus of contemporary life and at the same time a record of the history of society. Although it is the work of man it is also the creation of time. It would be unworthy of the heritage of man if care were not taken to conserve these traditional harmonies which constitute the core of man's own existence.

> The built vernacular heritage is important; it is the fundamental expression of the culture of a community, of its relationship with its territory and, at the same time, the expression of the world's cultural diversity.

Vernacular building is the traditional and natural way by which communities house themselves. It is a continuing process including necessary changes and continuous adaptation as a response to social and environmental constraints. The survival of this tradition is threatened world-wide by the forces of economic, cultural and architectural homogenisation. How these forces can be met is a fundamental problem that must be addressed by communities and also by governments, planners, architects, conservationists and by a multidisciplinary group of specialists."

A full copy of the charter is included in the Annex.

Regulatory limit
This is the score associated with the minimum changes required to ensure compliance with Building Regulations. It is possible to envisage a scenario where it is possible to create a satisfactory refurbishment in terms of conservation, environment and energy but which does not meet the requirements of regulations relating to acoustics and/or fire and so the scheme would not be acceptable. In this scenario some extra questions need to be asked as part of the methodology because if there is a requirement to comply with Building Regulations, and this is not feasible, then the whole idea of refurbishment is unacceptable and some alternative scheme would need to be designed.

It does not always seem to be clear exactly when Building Regulations apply to heritage buildings. The ODPM *Building Regulations explanatory booklet* (ODPM, 2005) states that compliance is required:

- if the repair work is significant, eg removing a substantial part of a wall and rebuilding it; underpinning a building; or replacing the roof with a heavier material or thatch (Approved Document A – *Structure*)
- if there is a material change of use – for example converting a house into flats or a non-dwelling place into a house. In this case 'the whole or part of the building must comply' with Building Regulations relating to:
    - escape and other fire precautions (Approved Document B *Fire safety)*
    - hygiene (Approved Document G *Hygiene*)
    - sound insulation (Approved Document E *Resistance to the passage of sound*)
    - conservation of energy (Approved Document L1B *Conservation of fuel and power* [existing dwellings] or Approved Document L2B *Conservation of fuel and power in buildings [other than existing dwellings]*).

Fire protection
There is a distinction to be made between issues that are potentially life threatening and ones that are more concerned with comfort or psychological well-being. For example, fire protection is obviously critical and much work has been done to find ways of meeting the performance requirements of Part B (*Fire safety*) without compromising what we value in an historic building. However, this can still result in difficulties – for example the incorporation of sprinkler systems into historic buildings (see Historic Scotland, 1998).

The promotion of an engineered approach to fire protection in relation to a thorough risk assessment for the building in question is one example of the change in the approach which has been developed by designers and others towards the Building Regulations, as the Regulations have moved away from prescribing solutions in favour of performance standards. For example a door may not need to withstand a fire well beyond the time that it actually takes to evacuate the building, provided that the means of escape is reinforced by a reliable fire detection and warning system.

Conservation of energy

The area that has provoked the greatest discussion was the conservation of energy. As a result the final versions of both Part L1 and Part L2 that came into effect in April 2006 contained specific guidance on historic buildings and the need to improve energy efficiency whilst not prejudicing the character of the building. Detailed guidance can be found in an interim guidance note produced by English Heritage (2004). Similar guidance is given in Part E (*Passage of sound*) where a balance between the need of the building and the requirement of sound insulation is advocated.

In particular, the 2006 version of Part L requires that, where there is a material change of use (for example alteration to a building so that it contains a greater or lesser number of dwellings than it did previously), work on controlled fittings and services (that is windows, door and lighting), work on controlled services (largely heating systems and controls), or work on thermal elements (particularly walls), then improvements should be made to the thermal efficiency of the equipment or elements. However, this requirement has a proviso that is important to pre-1919 houses:

> "Where it is not reasonable in the context of the scheme to achieve the performance set out in Table A1 (within the Approved Document) the level of performance achieved should be as close to this as practically possible."

There is a potential for conflict between conservation principles and regulations for thermal elements but this clause 55 states:

> "If such an upgrade is not technically or functionally feasible or would not achieve a simple pay back of 15 years or less, the element should be upgraded to the best standard that is technically and functionally feasible and which can be achieved within a simple payback of no greater than 15 years".

This requirement for thermal efficiency would not seem to give any limit if the project involves only refurbishment but if an extension is included then there may be some need to upgrade the rest of the house as part of this but Part L should be studied in detail in this case.

Sound insulation

Approved Document E (2003 edition) contains minimum performance standards for sound insulation that have to be achieved for compliance with the Building Regulations of England and Wales. Performance standards are given for new build dwellings and for dwelling houses and flats formed by a material change of use. A material change of use might be, for example, dividing (a) what was previously a single dwelling into separate flats or (b) converting a maisonette above ground floor business premises into separate dwellings. For (b), not only will walls and floors separating the newly formed dwellings need to achieve the minimum standards of sound insulation but the floor separating the ground floor business premises must achieve the minimum performance standard for airborne sound insulation. That is, the Building Regulations require that the floor separating the dwelling from the business premises must provide reasonable resistance to sound from the activities in the premises below. It is not a requirement under the Building Regulations that the business premises be protected from the dwelling above. It should be noted that the minimum standard of airborne sound insulation may not provide reasonable isolation from all activities, such as, playing music in bars.

Where, say, a Victorian terraced house is refurbished but the works carried out do not constitute a material change of use, it is unlikely that a building control body would require evidence of acoustic performance. However, refurbishments can affect the transmission of sound to adjacent properties. For example, if two downstairs rooms in a dwelling are converted to one through-room with floorboards to walk on and minimal soft furnishings, the sound transmission between adjacent properties may change.

Some older properties, including Victorian terraced or semi-detached houses, have separating walls comprising a single brick (approximately 114 mm or 4.5 inches) with plaster on both sides. During a major refurbishment it is worth considering improving the sound insulation of separating walls and it is reasonable to recommend improving the sound insulation of separating walls comprising a single brick. Guidance on relatively simple improvements can be found in a BRE leaflet *Improving sound insulation in homes* (www.bre.co.uk/pdf/soundins_homes.pdf), which describes fitting an independent lining to a separating wall.

Treatments other than those to separating walls may also be needed. Where floor joists are built into separating walls and are retained, it should be ensured that they are well sealed. Victorian domestic buildings often have solid masonry walls. Sometimes these external walls may be dry lined to improve their thermal insulation. Independent linings to external walls can also help to improve the sound insulation between dwellings. However, porous insulating materials, such as mineral wool help to absorb sound in cavities behind plasterboard. Closed cell lightweight polymer foam materials are unlikely to absorb sound in the same way although they may have desirable thermal properties.

When embarking on improvements to sound insulation between buildings it is useful to have a good idea of what levels of improvement might be achieved. Doubling the thickness of a solid masonry wall may improve its airborne sound insulation by 5 dB. A reduction in sound pressure level of 10 dB is generally accepted as being equivalent to halving loudness. Therefore, although improving sound insulation between dwellings can significantly improve privacy between dwellings it can be difficult to make improvements such that activities in adjacent properties cannot be heard. If particularly high sound insulation is required, expert advice from an appropriately qualified person is advisable.

Sustainability limit

The sustainability limit is more complex as the three components of sustainability – economy, environment and society – need to be considered.

- Economics are clearly important as there will be a point beyond which the refurbishment costs will exceed the benefits – where the most likely measure of benefits is the market value of the property or the income from letting. The expected benefits can be increased by the inclusion of indirect benefits – for example income to local shops – but this needs to be handled carefully as it is all too easy to predict benefits which are never actually captured. It is also possible to reduce the apparent costs by some form of grant or subsidy but if this is the case then its inclusion must be clearly stated.
- Environmental impacts can often dominate discussions of sustainability and it is clear that they are very important in any assessment and need to include not only carbon dioxide emissions but also other sources of pollution to the air, soil and water as well as the animals, plants and trees in the locality.
- Social impacts are the most difficult to quantify and so they are difficult to assess. In many schemes there are likely to be both positive and negative impacts – an unsuccessful scheme is likely to result in loss of community and no perceived bettering of the built environment. A well thought out scheme with community buy in could improve the sense of well being, security and contentment. But there is also the risk of a scheme being too successful in economic terms leading to gentrification and loss of the original community.

Relationships between limits

The position of the limits are likely to vary from location to location and also vary in their relative positions. Their relative positions will identify potential conflicts. Three examples of potential conflicts are:

● The regulatory limit is beyond the conservation limit:
In order to comply with Building Regulations some compromise will be required. In the case of a failure to comply with Part L (*Thermal performance*) there could be a relaxing of the requirements on the basis that the built heritage is involved. However, there will be other cases where regulations will need to dominate and more extensive work be carried out.

● The regulatory limit is beyond the economic limit:
In this case the regulatory limit is beyond the economic limit which means that the proposed scheme is uneconomic.

● The social limit is beyond the economic limit:
For this example the individual components of the sustainability limit have been separated to illustrate the situation where the social limit (or at least the requirements of the community) lies beyond the economic limit and so the aspiration and needs of the community cannot be met within the economic scope of the project.

Benchmarking pre-1919 housing using EcoHomes XBC: actions and impacts

The refurbishment of buildings can be visualised as a series of actions each of which alters the performance of the building and has the potential to improve the EcoHomes XBC rating. In conservation terms the actions can be equated with interventions and in the case of conservation the number and extent of the interventions is kept to a minimum. Using the scoring system it is possible to establish a baseline and quantify the effect of different actions (see Figure 1).

Current condition

Starting at the bottom left hand corner of Figure 1 the current condition is defined using the overall total score from Table 4 – a score of 11 which is below the start of the EcoHomes XBC rating scale. This assumes that the houses in question:

● are typical terraced houses with solid walls 225 mm thick in stone and/or brick
● have two party walls (for a mid-terrace) and a suspended floor
● have a pitched roof and are slated or tiled
● have typical dimensions of 3 m × 6.5 m with a rear kitchen extension 2 m × 4 m
● have single-glazed sash windows
● are heated by a gas fire in two ground floor rooms and electric storage heaters in two upstairs rooms
● have white goods that are more than 10 years old.

It is assumed that the locality is in an urban area served by public transport, with a small external space (garden or yard) typical of this type of location for each house, a drying line and water butt. It is also assumed that there is a normal provision of waste collection including some provision for recycling. It is assumed that this situation will continue for the foreseeable future – the no refurbishment option (Scenario 1 in Table 4).

Action 1

This first action involves only the regeneration of the locality and is the same as Scenario 2 in Table 4. The actions envisaged are typical of those which would occur as part of a regeneration/renewal scheme within an urban environment.

The actions include:

- provision and adoption of an energy policy and a commitment to a reduction in energy consumption
- provision of energy efficiency advice
- provision and adoption of an environmental policy and a commitment to protect ecological features during maintenance and refurbishment work
- an open tenant consultation on energy and environmental issues
- giving advice to the tenants/occupants on the purchasing of energy efficient white goods
- providing advice on operating the heating system controls has been provided to individual householders
- providing energy efficient external lighting in communal areas
- making pedestrian routes to local amenities safer
- provision of a policy to positively enhance the ecology of the locality
- provision of maintenance specifications which protect the local environment
- preparing a written policy to support the recycling of materials.

All of these actions can be undertaken as part of a renewal scheme and do not directly affect the buildings though they may well affect the appearance of the townscape and improve the sense of well being of those living in the area.

Conservation versus restoration

At some point the extent of the work required will mean that the project really changes from conservation to restoration, as it is no longer the repair of existing materials but the larger scale replacement of the fabric, and a much greater range of internal reconstruction/alteration. It is suggested that this point is reached when less than 80% of the original fabric and fittings of the building are retained in the refurbishment work but this may vary between projects. It is likely that the changes will be internal as described in Action 3.

Action 2

This represents a very basic upgrading of the houses – initially to the Decent Homes standard (ODPM, 2004). This standard requires the property to meet or exceed the current statutory minimum requirements for the state of repair of the property, the facilities and services, and for a reasonable degree of thermal comfort. The commitment to the first three items will tend to improve the condition of the property and the overall appearance of the locality but it is only the last one – the provision of an efficient central heating system and some roof space insulation – which will have a direct effect on the eco-score. The requirements for thermal comfort are given in Table 5.

Table 5 Summary of the requirements for identifying a Decent Home based on thermal comfort*	
Decent Homes criterion	**Primary data required**
Does it provide a reasonable degree of thermal comfort at affordable cost? (ie does it have effective insulation and heating?)	● Has it gas or oil programmable central heating or electric storage heaters/LDG/programmable sold fuel central heating or similarly efficient heating system? ● For gas/oil programmable heating: has it cavity wall insulation and/or at least 50 mm of roof insulation, where appropriate? ● For electric storage heaters/LPG/programmable solid fuel central heating: has it cavity wall insulation and at least 200 mm of roof insulation, where appropriate?

* Taken from Table 4 in *Decent Homes: Capturing the standard at the local level. A supplementary annex to collecting, managing and using housing stock information – a good practice guide*. DTLR 2000.

Action 3

The important work for Action 3 will include:

- the provision of a conservation plan for the properties
- a commitment and implementation of policies for refurbishment, on the use of timber from sustainable sources or re-use of timber, and limitations on the impact of the other materials generated and used during the refurbishment
- improvements in the energy efficiency of the properties by the use of more energy efficient appliances to reduce the emissions of carbon dioxide, for example the installation of a condensing boiler, and the installation of loft insulation and draught reduction measures
- provision of new bathroom fixtures and fittings, for example dual flush toilets and showers.

It is not envisaged that it will include changes to the fabric and appearance of the property, for example the installation of replacement windows or external insulation systems.

It is important to note that these are all changes within the building and so they are unlikely to change the external appearance. The changes would be covered by Part L of the Building Regulations and there is a requirement that the new heating system is at least as good as the one being replaced. Of course if possible, it would be sensible if the new system and appliances were better and as efficient as is reasonable within cost and space constraints.

Action 4

The increased scale of the changes allows the eco-rating to be improved beyond fair to good by the provision of a much greater range of energy and environmentally efficient fittings, for example:

- improvements in the energy efficiency of the properties by the use of more energy efficient appliances to reduce the emissions of carbon dioxide, such as the installation of a condensing boiler, and loft insulation, draught reduction measures and provision of new radiators
- provision of new bathroom fixtures and fittings, for example dual flush toilets and showers
- the structural alteration of the property to incorporate these new fixtures and fittings
- some windows may be replaced with more energy efficient units.

Some of these changes could have been carried out as part of Action 3 but in Action 4 the changes are likely to be more comprehensive.

The inclusion of structural alterations may allow improvement to be made in the thermal elements as defined in Part L – for example:

- the provision of 250 mm of insulation in the roof space
- the fitting of insulation between floor joists
- the dry lining/insulation of the internal face of external walls.

It is not envisaged that the work undertaken as conservation and that undertaken as restoration are exclusive but that the scope and extent of the work is much greater when the work is seen as restoration.

At some point the provision of segregated domestic recycling facilities should be included – either in each house or more likely in the external space.

Conservation limit

At some point the extent of the work will mean that the conservation limit will have been reached. This is defined as the point beyond which conservation principles and good practice will become compromised if further changes are made to the building, for example the replacement of windows in a conservation area, the replacement of an historic roof with photovoltaic panels, or the application of an external rendering system. If the building is listed there may also be limits on internal alterations, for example the dry lining of the walls to improve thermal performance. This limit could come at almost any point on Figure 1, depending on the restriction placed on the building by its statutory listing or location.

Action 5

These are the actions and interventions that could take place beyond the conservation limit and so would include those described as unacceptable in the box above headed Conservation limit.

Sustainability limit

In the same way that it is possible to define a conservation limit, it is possible to define a sustainability limit – though this latter limit is potentially far more complex with social and environmental needs as well as economics to be considered (see text under heading Sustainability limit on page 13). The needs and wishes of society, particularly those most closely associated with the building or its immediate environs, could result in the extent of the actions resulting in what is perceived as an unacceptable environmental impact. For example, the creation of additional parking spaces at the expenses of existing open spaces or ecological habitats.

But it is more likely that the limit will be financial – that is, the amount of investment required to achieve a certain eco-rating or improvement in energy efficiency cannot be justified in terms of the likely returns. This is always likely to be a problem in areas where there is limited demand for this type of housing. If it is agreed that if a higher eco-rating is required then it is likely that some form of subsidy will be required to redress the market limitation.

It is possible for the conservation limit to be to the right of the sustainability limit in Figure 1 – this would reflect a situation where the cost of work to bring the building up to a certain standard using conservation techniques is not economically viable but where the use of modern materials and techniques could achieve a higher eco-score. This would be a difficult problem to resolve as it would require a degree on compromise and/or relaxation of conservation restrictions.

A particularly difficult situation would arise where the conservation limit was below that required to meet social needs – that is, the house would not be saleable – or was unacceptable in environmental terms – for example, where it is not possible to improve the thermal performance sufficiently because of conservation requirements restricting the use of internal and external insulation systems. This could leave a situation where the house could not be used but neither could it be improved any further for habitation.

Action 6
This is restricted to actions above the sustainability limit and above the conservation limit which are seen as necessary for some reason or reasons. It is difficult to think of an example that might occur in the real world but it could include the retention of some building or the facade of the building for structural reasons when it is not sustainable in conservation or sustainability terms.

Demolition
Although not identified on the diagram in Figure 1 there will always be some pressure to demolish a building or group of buildings for a number of reasons. The most likely reason put forward will be that it is uneconomic to bring the building up to a standard that will be acceptable in terms of meeting the needs and expectations of the occupants. This could be extended to cases where it is not possible to reach a required eco-rating and the extension of this concept could lead to demolishing large areas because much greater energy efficiency can be achieved in replacement properties. This is the approach advocated in the Oxford ECI *40% House* report which was published in 2005 and which is being used on some Pathfinder projects. In terms of sustainability and conservation it should be seen as a last resort and only considered if there are no other options. However, there will be many occasions where some demolition will be necessary in order for a project to be sustainable it terms of the provision of suitable accommodation units, the provision of parking, and the provision of open spaces and parks.

Identifying the key actions in the refurbishment of pre-1919 housing

1 Define the conservation limit – are any of the buildings listed? Are all or some of the houses in a conservation area?
2 Define the sustainability limit – what does the community want? Expect? What is the market value of the existing houses? What is the likely value of a refurbished house? Does the project include housing association, local authority or registered social landlord housing? Is the project to be commercial? Are there any environmental limits? Are there any protected sites?
3 Is the refurbishment of the houses part of a wider regeneration scheme? What improvements could be made to the locality? Can these be measured using EcoHomes XBC?
4 How are the buildings constructed? What is their current condition? Does the condition vary?
5 Estimate the Decent Homes EcoHomes XBC score – do the houses reach this level already?
6 Estimate the minimum acceptable EcoHomes XBC score that will make the houses both habitable and of a standard which people will want to occupy.
7 Agree the no change baseline.
8 Estimate the likely EcoHomes XBC score for:
    – Scenario 1: The house(s) and area as currently found
    – Scenario 2: The same house(s) with the area improved as part of a regeneration plan
    – Scenario 3: The house(s) refurbished to an agreed limit (for example the conservation limit) but with no regeneration of the area
    – Scenario 4: The house(s) refurbished and the area improved as part of a regeneration plan.

It is also possible to take a different approach and agree a target EcoHomes XBC rating – for example Very Good, and then examine the actions and interventions required to reach this target. There may well be a number of different plans that can reach the target. These can be compared and the most appropriate chosen, for example the lowest cost option or the one that retains the greatest amount of the townscape.

9 Estimate the percentage improvement or the increase in the eco-score as a measure of the improvement for each scenario.

10 Consider the whole life costs for each scenario including direct and indirect costs and benefits – but remembering that a benefit is not a benefit unless it can be captured.

11 Decide on a way forward.

Case study 1
The Nelson Housing Market Regeneration Scheme

Background

Nelson, the Lancashire town named after Admiral Lord Nelson, has many shops and businesses and is the seat of Pendle Borough Council (Figure 2). It was formed by the combination of Great and Little Marsden in the early 19th century and grew rapidly as a textile mill town. Marsden Hall, the former 16th century residence of the Walton family is located close to the town centre, though it has now been partly demolished.

The challenges that housing market renewal in Nelson needed to try to overcome include:

- an oversupply of terraced houses
- a backlog of investment in housing leading to a high number of unfit properties
- deterioration of conditions within residential neighbourhoods
- a declining town centre
- lack of facilities
- poor private sector landlords
- low quality employment opportunities
- poor educational attainment.

Figure 2 View of the Whitefield area of Nelson, from Noggarth. St Mary's church is on the right and the Leeds and Liverpool canal and M65 are in the foreground (by permission of Andrew Stringer)

A public inquiry was held in January 2002 over Pendle Borough Council's plan to declare a clearance area in the Whitefield district of Nelson. The proposals included the purchase, demolition and redevelopment of 160 Victorian mill workers houses. Towards the end of 2002 the inquiry found in favour of the retention of the houses. However, the ODPM asked the inquiry to be re-opened in 2003 to consider whether the retention of the houses was still viable in the current housing market in the area. The inquiry again found in favour of the residents and a new regeneration plan was developed. In November 2004 the Prince's Foundation for the Built Environment held an Enquiry by Design (EBD) – which provided a forum for consultations with many stakeholders. A copy of the presentation on the EBD and the final report can be found at www.pendle.gov.uk/site/scripts/documents_info.php?document ID= 220&pageNumber=3.

The EBD included the development of an overall plan for the Whitefield area, which is shown in Figure 3.

A number of Priority Action Areas were identified and agreed in Nelson:

- Whitefield Priority Action Area
- Nelson Town Centre
- Bradley Priority Action Area
- Southfield Priority Action Area.

In November 2005 the Whitefield Regeneration Partnership was established to coordinate activities and oversee improvements in the Whitefield area. The partnership was made up of representatives from different agencies, heritage organisations and local residents.

Alongside this, the Whitefield Community Forum was established in December 2005. The Forum brought together people from across the Whitefield area so that their views could be fed into the Whitefield Regeneration Partnership. Forum meetings took place on a regular basis with all residents of Whitefield welcome to attend.

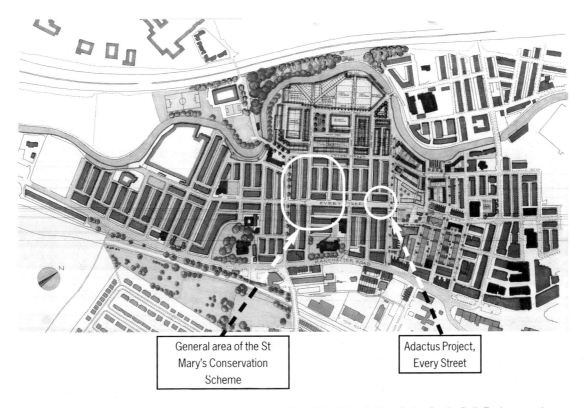

General area of the St Mary's Conservation Scheme

Adactus Project, Every Street

Figure 3 The overall master plan for the Whitefield area (by permission of the Prince's Foundation for the Built Environment)

In April 2006 it was announced that the winners of the Whitefield Design Competition run by RIBA and CABE (Commission for Architecture and the Built Environment) were Maccreanor Lavington/R.gen. Their ideas for Whitefield included proposals for:

- bringing more than 100 empty houses back into use through refurbishment and imaginative conversions of two properties into one – a choice popular with residents in the area where there are many extended families
- building more than 80 new homes
- ensuring new and refurbished homes are green and energy-efficient with average fuel bills of less than £50 per year
- providing a range of new community facilities for all of Nelson including a new community centre
- a major public square as the focus of the new community
- reconnecting Whitefield with the centre of Nelson, the canal and the surrounding landscape.

The winning team pledged to work closely with residents, neighbours and partners in setting up a project base in Whitefield. At the same time Pendle Borough Council was committed to working with current residents to help them stay in the area and buy into new or improved properties, as well as encouraging people living outside the area to move in.

By the middle of 2006 one renewal scheme had been completed in the St Mary's Area of Whitefield and a second project started in Every Street. The two projects provide an interesting contrast as they represent two quite different approaches to the improvement of the existing housing.

The Housing Market Renewal Scheme – St Mary's Conservation Area

In the St Mary's Conservation Area, a £3.9 million Group Repair Scheme has been completed with funding from the ELEVATE Housing Market Renewal Scheme (Figures 4 and 5). ELEVATE East Lancashire is one of the government's nine housing market renewal pathfinders. It is charged with finding innovative solutions to the problem of low demand, negative equity, and housing market collapse in towns across East Lancashire.

The renewal scheme was described as an enveloping scheme as the emphasis was on the external fabric of the properties. Most of the properties were in private ownership and occupied at the time of the scheme. The scheme included:

- fitting traditional double glazed sash windows to improve energy efficiency
- re-laying the roofs and the insulating of the roof spaces
- use of traditional materials and original design features for the chimney stacks which are in keeping with the period of the houses
- replacement of front doors and rainwater goods
- cleaning and re-pointing of the external masonry
- refurbishment of boundary walls and gates to improve the overall appearance of the area.

In some houses a limited amount of work was carried out internally, for example the replacement of rotten floor joists.

A total of 180 properties were originally scheduled for improvement under this scheme but it is likely that there will be sufficient funds for around 120 houses. As it is a Market Renewal Scheme the intention was that the scheme will have a positive impact on the area as a whole and not just on the properties involved.

The cost of the work varied between £28,000 and £32,000 per house depending on the extent of the work needed.

From available data on house prices it appears that the investment has, in general, been successful in financial terms. The sale prices recorded over the two years from 2004 to 2006 show a rise from around £25,000 for a two-bed house prior to refurbishment to around £55,000. Properties in the area that were originally scheduled for demolition have a much lower market value – around £10,000 to £15,000 – but they need considerably more work to bring them up to standard. Interestingly some properties in the same streets seem to have had a higher value for a number of years – perhaps reflecting an earlier investment of money.

This approach to renewal has an emphasis on the appearance of the houses and their external envelope. It assumes that a more buoyant housing market will result in greater investment by owners inside their homes (for example efficient central heating systems and white goods) and in the locality by the local authority.

Figure 4 Terrace of houses refurbished as part of the St Mary's Conservation Area

Figure 5 A view in St Mary's Conservation Area showing the stark contrast between the refurbished houses (on the right) and the adjacent streets

In terms of the EcoHomes XBC scoring system, the type of refurbishment would improve the thermal performance and receive credits for the use of materials (assuming that much of the original material is kept). This would be sufficient to achieve a Fair rating but without a wider regeneration scheme for the locality – and a programme of guidance and education on the upgrading of the properties, the use of energy efficient fixtures and fittings, and the recycling of waste – it will be difficult to achieve a higher rating. However, the refurbishment does potentially allow the retention of many original features within the houses and maintains the appearance of the streetscape within the conservation area. It does appear that house prices have increased to reflect the investment during the period 2004 to 2006.

The Adactus Project – Every Street

The Housing Association, Adactus, commenced work in April 2006 to refurbish a short terrace of houses in Every Street (Figures 6 and 7). The members of the Adactus Housing Group build, renovate and manage affordable housing for rent and sale. The Group's principal subsidiaries are housing associations, legally known as registered social landlords, and regulated by the Housing Corporation.

The Adactus Housing Group was formed in August 2002 although its members trace their origins back to the 1960s. It owns and manages over 6,200 homes across 17 local authority areas in the north west of England, employs 337 staff and has an annual turnover in excess of £22 million.

In 2004 Adactus completed a very successful project in Preston where it refurbished a number of rundown terraced houses in the Frenchwood area to provide contemporary open plan one bedroom homes with a full height atrium and a new steel frame structure whilst largely retaining the external appearance of the properties. When the project started in 2003 the houses cost £20,000 and the work on each one £45,000. The selling price was £75,000 to buy on a shared ownership basis or £240 per month to rent.

The project in Nelson was along similar lines showing how old houses can be given a new inside layout and design style which suits modern living. Adactus bought seven houses from Pendle Borough Council for £1 and created two end of terrace houses with three bedrooms. This was achieved by knocking two houses together at each end of the terrace and creating three single bedroom units in the remaining three houses. It is expected that the larger units will sell for £95,000 and the smaller ones for £50,000 – prices that are consistent with local market prices. Work started in April 2006 and is due for completion in late 2006.

The work to each house was far more extensive than for the St Mary's Conservation Area project which allowed the potential for greater improvements in the thermal performance and efficiency of the fixtures and fittings. There was still a requirement for a wider regeneration scheme for the locality, but it would be possible to provide a programme of guidance and education on policies and actions to improve sustainability as part of a buyer's pack. The negative side was a reduction in the re-use of materials as a result of the more extensive demolition unless a plan for the salvaging and re-use of the materials was implemented. In terms of conservation principles there was far less potential for the retention of original features – though the streetscape will remain largely unaltered.

Potentially this project could achieve a Good or Better rating but this would depend on the use of sustainable materials and the extent to which materials can be salvaged or recycled during the refurbishment work.

Figure 6 Terrace of seven houses being refurbished by Adactus in Every Street, Nelson

Figure 7 Rear elevation of the Adactus houses in Every Street showing the extensive nature of the refurbishment including the demolition of the original rear extensions

Scope for further improvements in refurbishments in Nelson

The two projects completed, or nearing completion, in Nelson have demonstrated that the current housing stock in the Whitefield area is extremely adaptable and that it can be refurbished to a standard which makes the project economically viable. The more extensive refurbishment in Every Street has the potential to provide very energy efficient houses with interesting internal spaces but they clearly go beyond the conservation limit and are likely to produce significant amounts of waste and require extensive use of modern materials with a potentially high environment impact.

However, it is possible to envisage two different approaches which could reduce the environmental impact whilst maintaining a more conservation based approach. The first is to consider the use of a district heating system based on a biomass boiler. This would be carbon neutral or very close to neutral even if the individual houses were not insulated to the very highest standards. The installation of this system would require changes in the infrastructure, but if this were undertaken as part of the overall regeneration of the area then it would be less difficult.

The potential environmental impact could be further reduced by combining the use of carbon neutral technology with a planned re-use of construction materials supplemented by low environmental impact traditional materials such as lime mortars, insulation made from sheep's wool or newspaper, and timber.

Case study 2
The Flagship Home Project, Beaufort Gardens, London

36 Beaufort Gardens, Knightsbridge, London is a five-storey Victorian terrace house comprising of bed-sits and one self-contained flat. It is representative of a large proportion of the housing stock in the Royal Borough of Kensington and Chelsea, other boroughs in London and other British cities. It is in a conservation area but is not a listed building.

The Flagship Home Project took this typical five storey Victorian terraced house and refurbished it to maximise energy efficiency and reduce CO_2 emissions.

The house was refurbished to maximise energy efficiency to reduce emissions of CO_2. The aim of the project was to demonstrate that this can make a positive contribution to a low carbon economy while maintaining the traditional character of the building and adhering to planning contraints. (A low carbon economy is one that does not use a lot of energy in the manufacturing process.) For example, the refurbishment used low carbon products like wooden windows rather than u-PVC.

Figure 8 The front elevation of the refurbished Flagship Project house in Kensington, London (by permission of the Flagship Project)

The objectives of the project were:
● to demonstrate and promote practicable, cost effective, energy efficiency measures to private landlords
● to target older, solid walled properties in conservation areas that have been ignored by national and regional campaigns for the reduction of energy use in the past
● to demonstrate how older properties can make a positive contribution to a low carbon economy through the use of innovative methods used in conjunction with traditional sustainable green materials
● to encourage a close working relationship and a better understanding between statutory bodies and building preservation organisations
● to tackle issues such as fuel poverty that may be alleviated through more energy efficient housing
● to provide the Royal Borough of Kensington and Chelsea and Westminster City Councils with the opportunity to explore new innovative measures, identify new ways of working and promote sustainable housing
● to use the property as an exhibition home to promote innovative energy solutions to our target audience.

At the start of the project the property was classed as 'hard to treat' and in addition to the solid brick walls it had high ceilings, large windows and no fixed heating system.

The refurbished house is now in multiple occupation (HMO) and consists of 18 bed-sits and one self-contained flat. It provides accommodation for 36 tenants. The landlord has agreed, in accordance with Section 106 of the Town & Country Planning Act, to let a quarter of the bed-sits (two double, and two single) to key workers (teachers, social workers) on affordable rents (two-thirds of the market rent).

The changes made to the property include the provision of dry lining, double glazed windows in the rear elevation, and secondary glazing in the front elevation where the aesthetic appearance was considered more important.

Two condensing boilers were installed to provide communal heating to all the units but with each tenant having radiators and programmable controls. Solar panels were installed on the roof to supply part of the building's hot water with a heat recovery ventilation system.

A new top floor has been added to the house – providing three more bedsits available for rent. This was approved by the Royal Borough of Kensington and Chelsea's Planning Department as similar work had already been carried out on other properties in the same street, providing precedent for planning permission. The addition of a new storey meant that a new roof could be added, highly insulated in compliance with the Building Regulations.

Planning an effective ventilation strategy for the building proved problematic. This was due to the difficulties associated with accommodating ductwork within the revised building layout and the restriction of not taking any extract or inlets through the front facade (for conservation reasons).

These problems were resolved by installing one mechanical ventilation with heat recovery unit per floor and in a number of cases providing a single individual unit within a bedsit.

The light fittings only take low energy light bulbs and the white goods are all A-rated for energy efficiency.

Combining these changes in the refurbishment project has significantly reduced energy consumption and CO_2 emissions. For example:
● energy costs have fallen by 67% from approximately £3,400 to £1,100 per year
● CO_2 emissions have been cut by 63% from a level of 25.74 tonnes per year to 9.58 tonnes
● after the work was completed the houses national home energy rating (NHER) increased from approximately 3.0 to 9.0.

Case study 3
The Nottingham Ecohome

The Nottingham Ecohome is a self managed sustainable refurbishment undertaken by Penney Poyzer (broadcaster and author in environmental issues), and Gil Schalom, (architect specialising in conservation and sustainability), and Global Action Plan.

The house, dating from around 1898, was in a run-down state, having been a student house for 20 years. It cost £84,500 in 1998. It had good transport connections and was close to a wide range of amenities.

The project set out to create a good example of eco retrofit, with every element as good as could be achieved using low impact materials. The project priorities were to:
- upgrade thermal performance: insulate as highly as possible/practical
- try to retain thermal mass
- recover heat from ventilation
- improve air tightness
- experiment with different low-impact materials
- be as autonomous as possible in: energy, water, sewage treatment and food
- reduce CO_2 emissions to a minimum, demonstrating that our older houses can be made energy efficient.

Figure 9 The front elevation of the Nottingham Ecohome after completion of the refurbishment (by permission of Penney Poyzer and Gil Schalom)

Figure 10 Rear elevation of the Nottingham Ecohome showing external render insulation (by permission of Penney Poyzer and Gil Schalom)

Table 6 Energy efficiency measures at the Nottingham Ecohome

	Existing U-value	Good practice U-value	Predicted U-value	Description of work undertaken
Roof/loft space				
Roof insulation above the ceiling	1.9	0.20	0.10	400 mm of Warmcell recycled newspaper insulation above and between the ceiling joists
Roof insulation along slope of rafters	–	0.30	0.12	300 mm of blown Warmcell insulation in a plywood web
Additional work				Re-roofed re-using most of old slates; Installed breathable underlay to protect insulation; Extended verge overhang for future external insulation
Floors				
Solid ground floor	0.7	0.30–0.35	0.18	Excavated down and laid damp proof membrane horizontally and vertically to above ground level; 150 mm polystyrene with 50 mm edge upstands; 100 mm concrete slab
Suspended ground floor	0.7	0.30–0.35	0.23	100 mm of sheep's wool between the joists and 60 mm of insulating wood fibre board (Gutex) beneath the joists. A breather membrane over the Gutex
Second floor				Existing floorboards taken up and the joists strengthened; Loose Rockwool placed between joists for sound insulation (should have used sheep's wool but not readily available at the time); 3 mm Regupol sheet made of recycled rubber and cork over joists for impact noise reduction; Existing boards replaced and supplemented with additional reclaimed boards to enlarged the floor area
External walls				
External insulation	2.1	0.35	0.23	140 mm expanded polystyrene board and a Sto render system. The thermal performance of the walls has been improved by 860%
Internal insulation	2.1	0.35	0.20	2 × 50 mm zero odp phenolic foam laminate boards (This was applied to the front elevation so that the external appearance could be maintained)
Windows	4.7			Single glazed
		2.9		Good practice for secondary glazing
		2.0		Good practice for double glazing
			1.3–1.5	Soft low e coatings, argon filled double glazed units and plastic spacers NB: The house would originally have had single glazing – double glazed u-PVC windows were inherited and no secondary glazing. Two north facing sets of French windows were triple glazed, krypton filled with two low e coats
Doors		2.0 or less	1.3–1.5	Replacement of some of the existing u-PVC doors with fsc timber
Ventilation				
				Both bathrooms and both kitchens have heat recovery fans which save up to 80% of airborne heat. Whole house heat recovery mechanical ventilation
Energy sources				
				4 m² flat plate solar panel contributes 50% to annual hot water; wood-fired boiler for central heating and hot water top-up; 1100 litre accumulator stores and distributes hot water to the radiators and domestic use; It was planned to install one or two 1 metre diameter wind turbines (this is no longer the case as it would not generate viable amounts in this area; Renewable energy and low energy construction has saved £800 to £1000 a year

Over a period of six years the house was completely refurbished and documentation completed. The work carried out to improve energy efficiency, and energy and costs, is summarised in Tables 6 and 7.

Although the project has been completed, refurbishment is ongoing. A low energy kitchen is being installed and a contemporary garden is being created based on permaculture principles. There are also plans to install a new front door and create an insulated porch. Over time, the u-PVC windows will be replaced as the glazing units fail. The importance of energy efficient appliances and lighting are stressed: this is often more appropriate and cost effective than installing renewable electricity generation in an urban location.

Further details can be found at:

- www.msarch.co.uk/ecohome
- www.sustainablehousing.org.uk/documents/NottinghamRefurbishment.pdf
- http://projects.bre.co.uk/partL_study/pdf/Nottingham%20Ecohome.pdf.

Other measures to reduce the environmental impact:

- rainwater is collected off the roof and diverted into storage in the cellar storage tanks (total volume 400 litres). The down pipe diverters also filter grit and leaves. The water is automatically fed to WCs, washing machine and outside tap; it automatically tops up with mains when running low. This saves up to 50% on mains water
- composting chamber for dealing with solid part of human waste.
- dual low flush WCs, flushing at 2 and 4 litres compared to 9 or 7.5 litres in older style WCs
- 25 mm thick clay, reed and Hessian have been used as an alternative to plasterboard throughout main bathroom. This gives a high thermal mass that is and breathable and hygroscopic
- clay and sand self coloured plasters that need no painting used in some rooms
- different eco paints used from powder self mix casein to soya or citrus based emulsions
- birch ply shower enclosure and 100% natural linoleum floor in the main bathroom.

The overall energy savings are 75% in terms of costs and 85% in terms of tonnes of CO_2 emitted. Almost all of the savings come in the form of more efficient heating and hot water. The use of many natural materials lowers the environmental impact and is also likely to improve the internal atmosphere of the house. The project has been willing to use modern, more energy demanding materials where the benefits justify this choice, for example the use of expanded polystyrene to improve the insulation of the walls and solid floors.

Table 7 Energy and costs at the Nottingham Ecohome*

	Heating	Hot water	Cooking	Lights and appliances	Total
Original specification (before windows were replaced)					
£/year	2513	538	31	424	3569
GJ/year	113.4	24.3	6.3	19.1	163
CO_2 t/year	13.0	2.8	0.3	2.2	18.9
Actual figures (May 2005)					
£/year	250	122	79	388	867
GJ/year	49.4	24.1	3.6	17.5	94.6
CO_2 t/year	0.3	0.2	0.4	2.0	2.9
Aspirational (airtightness complete and windows upgraded)					
£/year	163	122	79	387	780
GJ/year	32.2	24.1	3.6	17.5	77.3
CO_2 t/year	0.2	0.2	0.4	2.0	2.8

* Figures based on NHER energy modelling and taken from www.sustainablehousing.org.uk/documents/NottinghamRefurbishment.pdf.

Conclusions

The technical, economic, environmental and social implications of retaining homes built in the UK between 1840 and 1919 have been extensively researched as part of this project. This project was designed to inform developers' decisions on whether and how to renovate Victorian and Edwardian houses. Renovating and refurbishing older housing stock involves complex decision-making. As well as being economically viable to restore, preferably within conservation good practice, the resulting homes need to be energy efficient and easy to maintain. They need to be located in areas where people want to live and where there are adequate transport links and social infrastructure such as shops and schools.

Sustainability has been the main focus of the project, both in terms of the materials and technologies used for renovation and refurbishment, and the ongoing economic and environmental effects of living in the houses after refurbishment. Heating, lighting and sanitation, for example, must meet or exceed the best modern standards if the houses are going to compete with newly built houses.

The project demonstrated that it is possible to establish a methodology that can be used to support decision making by establishing a benchmark from which the benefits of various actions can be objectively assessed using a scoring developed from EcoHomes XB. The methodology can also show that limits for both conservation and sustainability – whether economic, environmental and social – can be defined beyond which actions become unacceptable in terms of damage to the built heritage or in purely economic terms. By documenting case studies in Nelson, Nottingham and London the project has shown that a range of refurbishment schemes can be successful in environmental and economic terms, but that in a market-driven economy there are limits to what can be achieved. It has also highlighted the importance of considering a range of schemes and proceeding with the most appropriate one for that location, with an overall regeneration programme that meets the needs of the existing local community.

All the actions relating to individual houses need to be undertaken as part of a wider regeneration scheme which includes not only improvements in the immediate environment but a programme of education and guidance on energy efficient measures, reducing water consumption and the positive management of the built heritage such that it benefits those living within its environs and those further afield.

The need for a wider programme of actions within the community raises a number of potential problems – particularly relating to responsibility for the programme and who bears the cost. If the houses are the responsibility of a housing association, registered social landlord or the local authority, as are many of those in Whitefield, then there can be a central responsibility for implementing the project. However, if the houses are in private ownership then it is more difficult to achieve a coherent plan of internal and external improvements and so it may well take a number of years before the full benefits are seen as it is likely to be largely market driven.

References

DTLR. Decent Homes: Capturing the standard at the local level. A supplementary annex to collecting, managing and using housing stock information – a good practice guide. 2000. www.communities.gov.uk/pub/216/CapturingthestandardatthelocallevelPDF134Kb _id1152216.pdf.

English Heritage (2004). Building Regulations and historic buildings. Balancing the needs of energy conservation with those of building conservation: an interim guidance note on the application of Part L. London, English Heritage. www.english-heritage.org.uk/ server/show/ conWebDoc.3417.

English Heritage (2005). Conservation principles for the sustainable management of the historic environment. www.english-heritage.org.uk/upload/pdf/Conservation_Principles _A4%5B1%5D.pdf.

Environmental Change Institute (ECI) (2005). The 40% house report. Oxford, ECI. www.40percent.org.uk.

Historic Scotland (1998).The installation of sprinkler systems in historic buildings. Technical advice note 14. Edinburgh, Historic Scotland.

Office for National Statistics. General household survey 2004–2005.

Northern Ireland Statistics and Research Agency. Continuous household survey 2004–2005.

BRE

Anderson J, Mills K (2002). Refurbishment or redevelopment of office buildings? Sustainability comparisons. BRE Information Paper IP9/02 Part 1. Garston, BRE Bookshop.

Anderson J, Mills K (2002). Refurbishment or redevelopment of office buildings? Sustainability case histories. BRE Information Paper IP9/02 Part 2. Garston, BRE Bookshop.

EcoHomes XB: The environmental rating for existing housing. Assessment guidance notes. 2006. The guidance 2006. www.breeam.org.

Improving sound insulation in homes. www.bre.co.uk/pdf/soundins_homes.pdf.

Energy Saving Trust

Good practice case studies 315. Energy efficient refurbishment of solid walled houses. www.est.org.uk/bestpractice/publications/index.jsp.

Good practice case studies 316. Energy efficient refurbishment of solid walled flats. www.est.org.uk/bestpractice/publications/index.jsp.

Good practice case studies 418. Energy efficient refurbishment of existing housing – case studies. www.est.org.uk/bestpractice/publications/index.jsp.

Good practice guide 155. Energy efficient refurbishment of existing housing. www.est.org.uk/bestpractice/publications/index.jsp.

ODPM (now the Department for Communities and Local Government)

Building Regulations 2000.

A decent home – The definition and guidance for implementation. 2004.

Building Regulations explanatory booklet. 2005.

Annex
The ICOMOS Charter on
Built Vernacular Heritage

INTERNATIONAL COUNCIL
ON MONUMENTS AND SITES **I C⬤M O S** CONSEIL INTERNATIONAL
DES MONUMENTS ET DES SITES

Ratified by the ICOMOS 12th General Assembly, in Mexico, October 1999.

INTRODUCTION

The built vernacular heritage occupies a central place in the affection and pride of all peoples. It has been accepted as a characteristic and attractive product of society. It appears informal, but nevertheless orderly. It is utilitarian and at the same time possesses interest and beauty. It is a focus of contemporary life and at the same time a record of the history of society. Although it is the work of man it is also the creation of time. It would be unworthy of the heritage of man if care were not taken to conserve these traditional harmonies which constitute the core of man's own existence.

The built vernacular heritage is important; it is the fundamental expression of the culture of a community, of its relationship with its territory and, at the same time, the expression of the world's cultural diversity.

Vernacular building is the traditional and natural way by which communities house themselves. It is a continuing process including necessary changes and continuous adaptation as a response to social and environmental constraints. The survival of this tradition is threatened world-wide by the forces of economic, cultural and architectural homogenisation. How these forces can be met is a fundamental problem that must be addressed by communities and also by governments, planners, architects, conservationists and by a multidisciplinary group of specialists.

Due to the homogenisation of culture and of global socio-economic transformation, vernacular structures all around the world are extremely vulnerable, facing serious problems of obsolescence, internal equilibrium and integration.

It is necessary, therefore, in addition to the Venice Charter, to establish principles for the care and protection of our built vernacular heritage.

GENERAL ISSUES

1.   Examples of the vernacular may be recognised by:

a) A manner of building shared by the community;

b) A recognisable local or regional character responsive to the environment;

c) Coherence of style, form and appearance, or the use of traditionally established building types;

d) Traditional expertise in design and construction which is transmitted informally;

e) An effective response to functional, social and environmental constraints;

f) The effective application of traditional construction systems and crafts.

2.   The appreciation and successful protection of the vernacular heritage depend on the involvement and support of the community, continuing use and maintenance.

3.   Governments and responsible authorities must recognise the right of all communities to maintain their living traditions, to protect these through all available legislative, administrative and financial means and to hand them down to future generations.

PRINCIPLES OF CONSERVATION

1.   The conservation of the built vernacular heritage must be earned out by multidisciplinary expertise while recognising the inevitability of change and development, and the need to respect the community's established cultural identity.

2.   Contemporary work on vernacular buildings, groups and settlements should respect their cultural values and their traditional character,

3.   The vernacular is only seldom represented by single structures, and it is best conserved by maintaining and preserving groups and settlements of a representative character, region by region.

4.   The built vernacular heritage is an integral part of the cultural landscape and this relationship must be taken into consideration m the development of conservation approaches.

5.   The vernacular embraces not only the physical form and fabric of buildings, structures and spaces, but the ways in which they are used and understood, and the traditions and the intangible associations which attach to them.

GUIDELINES IN PRACTICE

1.   Research and documentation

Any physical work on a vernacular structure should be cautious and should be preceded by a full analysis of its form and structure. This document should be lodged in a publicly accessible archive.

2.   Siting, landscape and groups of buildings

Interventions to vernacular structures should be carried out in a manner which will respect and maintain the integrity of the siting, the relationship to the physical and cultural landscape, and of one structure to another.

3.   Traditional building systems

The continuity of traditional building systems and craft skills associated with the vernacular is fundamental for vernacular expression, and essential for the repair and restoration of these structures. Such skills should be retained, recorded and passed on to new generations of craftsmen and builders in education and training.

4.   Replacement of materials and parts

Alterations which legitimately respond to the demands of contemporary use should be effected by the introduction of materials which maintain a consistency of expression, appearance, texture and form throughout the structure and a consistency of building materials.

5.   Adaptation

Adaptation and reuse of vernacular structures should be carried out in a manner which will respect the integrity of the structure, its character and form while being compatible with acceptable standards of living. Where there is no break in the continuous utilisation of vernacular forms, a code of ethics within the community can serve as a tool of intervention.

6.   Changes and period restoration

Changes over time should be appreciated and understood as important aspects of vernacular architecture. Conformity of all parts of a building to a single period, will not normally be the goal of work on vernacular structures.

7.   Training

In order to conserve the cultural values of vernacular expression, governments, responsible authorities, groups and organisations must place emphasis on the following:

a) Education programmes for conservators in the principles of the vernacular;

b) Training programmes to assist communities in maintaining traditional building systems, materials and craft skills;

c) Information programmes which improve public awareness of the vernacular especially amongst the younger generation.

d) Regional networks on vernacular architecture to exchange expertise and experiences.

CIAV:

Madrid, January 30, 1996,

Jerusalem, March 28, 1996

Mikkeli, February 26, 1998.

Santo Domingo, August 26, 1998.

ICOMOS: Stockholm, September 10, 1998

Source: www.international.icomos.org/charters/vernacular_e.htm

Other reports from BRE Trust
(formerly Foundation for the Built Environment)

FB1   **Subsidence damage to domestic buildings: lessons learned and questions remaining**
R M C Driscoll and M S Crilly
September 2000

FB2   **Potential implications of climate change in the built environment**
Hilary M Graves and Mark C Phillipson
December 2000

FB3   **Behaviour of concrete repair patches under propped and unpropped conditions: critical review of current knowledge and practices**
T D G Canisius and N Waleed
March 2000

FB4   **Construction site security and safety: the forgotten costs**
Bob Knights, Tim Pascoe and Alice Henchley
December 2002

FB5   **New fire design method for steel frames with composite floor slabs**
Colin Bailey
January 2003

FB6   **Lessons from UK PFI and real estate partnerships: drivers, barriers and critical success factors**
Tim Dixon, Alan Jordan, Andrew Marston, James Pinder and Gaye Pottinger
November 2003

FB7   **An audit of UK social housing innovation**
Keith Ross, James Honour and Fran Nowak
February 2004

FB8   **Effective use of fibre reinforced polymer materials in construction**
S M Halliwell and T Reynolds
March 2004

FB9   **Summertime solar performance of windows with shading devices**
Paul Littlefair
February 2005

FB10   **Putting a price on sustainability**
BRE Centre for Sustainable Construction and Cyril Sweett
May 2005

FB11   **Modern methods of house construction: a surveyor's guide**
Keith Ross
June 2005

FB12   **Crime opportunity profiling of streets (COPS): a quick crime analysis – rapid implementation approach**
J Oxley, P Reijnhoudt, P van Soomeren, C Beckford
November 2005